犀犀的煩惱

文／孟瑛如、王銘涵
圖／闇寧
英文翻譯／吳侑達

我是犀犀，
我有很多熱心
助人的朋友。

我ㄨㄛˇ要ㄧㄠˋ摸ㄇㄛ讀ㄉㄨˊ點ㄉㄧㄢˇ字ㄗˋ書ㄕㄨ時ㄕˊ，
他ㄊㄚ們ㄇㄣ˙會ㄏㄨㄟˋ急ㄐㄧˊ著ㄓㄜ˙想ㄒㄧㄤˇ要ㄧㄠˋ幫ㄅㄤ我ㄨㄛˇ翻ㄈㄢ頁ㄧㄝˋ。

我ㄨㄛˇ要ㄧㄠˋ喝ㄏㄜ水ㄕㄨㄟˇ時ㄕˊ，
他ㄊㄚ們ㄇㄣ會ㄏㄨㄟˋ急ㄐㄧˊ著ㄓㄜ幫ㄅㄤ我ㄨㄛˇ打ㄉㄚˇ開ㄎㄞ水ㄕㄨㄟˇ杯ㄅㄟ。

上ㄕㄤ課ㄎㄜ時ㄕ，
他ㄊㄚ們ㄇㄣ會ㄏㄨㄟ好ㄏㄠ奇ㄑㄧ的ㄉㄜ不ㄅㄨ斷ㄉㄨㄢ碰ㄆㄥ觸ㄔㄨ
我ㄨㄛ的ㄉㄜ電ㄉㄧㄢ腦ㄋㄠ。

我要上廁所時，
他們會搶著要牽我走。

我很高興能夠擁有這樣一群朋友。他們讓我感到快樂！他們讓我的學校生活充實且滿足！

但我現在有一些煩惱的事，
不知道該如何開口跟朋友說。

每當我要行動的時候，
從四面八方伸過來的手，
常常會讓我搞不清楚方向。

每當我要離開座位時，
同學們忙著牽我，
他們不小心撞歪的桌椅，
常常讓我跌跌撞撞。

當老師上課說明翻到第幾頁時，同學們會不約而同的搶著幫我翻頁。他們的手指常會碰觸到點字，這樣會讓點字上的浮凸點消失，我就不能摸讀了，反而會找不到老師上課的進度。

我真的很感激身邊有
這群熱心的朋友。

但是，我希望他們能知道
我真正的需求。

我ㄨㄛˇ在ㄗㄞˋ入ㄖㄨˋ學ㄒㄩㄝˊ前ㄑㄧㄢˊ，
視ㄕˋ障ㄓㄤˋ巡ㄒㄩㄣˊ迴ㄏㄨㄟˊ老ㄌㄠˇ師ㄕ已ㄧˇ經ㄐㄧㄥ針ㄓㄣ對ㄉㄨㄟˋ我ㄨㄛˇ學ㄒㄩㄝˊ習ㄒㄧˊ
與ㄩˇ生ㄕㄥ活ㄏㄨㄛˊ的ㄉㄜˊ環ㄏㄨㄢˊ境ㄐㄧㄥ，　為ㄨㄟˋ我ㄨㄛˇ量ㄌㄧㄤˊ身ㄕㄣ訂ㄉㄧㄥˋ做ㄗㄨㄛˋ
了ㄌㄜˊ定ㄉㄧㄥˋ向ㄒㄧㄤˋ行ㄒㄧㄥˊ動ㄉㄨㄥˋ課ㄎㄜˋ程ㄔㄥˊ，　只ㄓˇ要ㄧㄠˋ周ㄓㄡ遭ㄗㄠ環ㄏㄨㄢˊ
境ㄐㄧㄥ的ㄉㄜˊ物ㄨˋ品ㄆㄧㄣˇ（　包ㄅㄠ含ㄏㄢˊ桌ㄓㄨㄛ椅ㄧˇ等ㄉㄥˇ）　不ㄅㄨˊ隨ㄙㄨㄟˊ
意ㄧˋ移ㄧˊ動ㄉㄨㄥˋ，　我ㄨㄛˇ都ㄉㄡ能ㄋㄥˊ行ㄒㄧㄥˊ動ㄉㄨㄥˋ自ㄗˋ如ㄖㄨˊ！

當我要行動時，
若你想幫我引導，

可以讓我扶著你的手
臂或是肩膀，我就能
隨著你身體的擺動，
辨識前進的方向！

當_{ㄉㄤ}我_{ㄨㄛ}在_{ㄗㄞ}摸_{ㄇㄛ}讀_{ㄉㄨ}點_{ㄉㄧㄢ}字_ㄗ書_{ㄕㄨ}時_ㄕ，
你_{ㄋㄧ}們_{ㄇㄣ}可_{ㄎㄜ}以_ㄧ用_{ㄩㄥ}口_{ㄎㄡ}頭_{ㄊㄡ}方_{ㄈㄤ}式_ㄕ提_{ㄊㄧ}醒_{ㄒㄧㄥ}我_{ㄨㄛ}，
我_{ㄨㄛ}就_{ㄐㄧㄡ}能_{ㄋㄥ}快_{ㄎㄨㄞ}速_{ㄙㄨ}找_{ㄓㄠ}到_{ㄉㄠ}正_{ㄓㄥ}確_{ㄑㄩㄝ}的_{ㄉㄜ}頁_{ㄧㄝ}數_{ㄕㄨ}。

我ㄨㄛˇ喜ㄒㄧˇ歡ㄏㄨㄢ你ㄋㄧˇ們ㄇㄣ˙，
喜ㄒㄧˇ歡ㄏㄨㄢ你ㄋㄧˇ們ㄇㄣ˙的ㄉㄜ˙陪ㄆㄟˊ伴ㄅㄢˋ，
喜ㄒㄧˇ歡ㄏㄨㄢ你ㄋㄧˇ們ㄇㄣ˙的ㄉㄜ˙熱ㄖㄜˋ情ㄑㄧㄥˊ，

喜ㄒㄧˇ歡ㄏㄨㄢ你ㄋㄧˇ們ㄇㄣ˙唸ㄋㄧㄢˋ故ㄍㄨˋ事ㄕˋ書ㄕㄨ給ㄍㄟˇ我ㄨㄛˇ聽ㄊㄧㄥ，
喜ㄒㄧˇ歡ㄏㄨㄢ你ㄋㄧˇ們ㄇㄣ˙跟ㄍㄣ我ㄨㄛˇ分ㄈㄣ享ㄒㄧㄤˇ生ㄕㄥ活ㄏㄨㄛˊ中ㄓㄨㄥ的ㄉㄜ˙喜ㄒㄧˇ怒ㄋㄨˋ哀ㄞ樂ㄌㄜˋ！
我ㄨㄛˇ真ㄓㄣ的ㄉㄜ˙好ㄏㄠˇ高ㄍㄠ興ㄒㄧㄥˋ擁ㄩㄥˇ有ㄧㄡˇ你ㄋㄧˇ們ㄇㄣ˙這ㄓㄜˋ一ㄧˋ群ㄑㄩㄣˊ朋ㄆㄥˊ友ㄧㄡˇ！

• 給教師及家長的話 •

　　首先感謝你打開這本書，相信你一定是想要為我們的視覺障礙學生做些什麼的關心者，我們才會藉由此書相遇。

　　視覺障礙教育的發展在臺灣已有很長的一段時間，隨著大家對「視覺障礙」的認識，溫馨的人們也都不吝於伸出雙手幫助他們。只是，有特殊需求的人們常因個人的障礙狀況與需求不同，所需要的適性需求協助也不一樣；有時候，「不適合」的幫助可能會造成他們更大的困擾。

　　因此，我們想藉由這本《犀犀的煩惱》提醒溫馨的人們，在熱情伸出雙手幫助前，可否先細心觀察與貼心體諒被幫助的人到底需要哪些幫忙？又該如何幫忙？若你想幫助身邊的視覺障礙朋友時，可以溫和的開口說：「你需要幫忙嗎？」或是說：「可以告訴我要如何做嗎？」如此一來，大家的幫助不會被打折扣，視覺障礙朋友也能得到真正的幫助與自在。

　　同時，我們也希望能藉由此書提醒視覺障礙學生可以主動開口尋求幫助，甚至告訴對方自己需要哪些適性協助。在「理解」與「同理」概念共同運作之下，社會就會更加祥和與溫暖。

　　本書另附有學習手冊，家長及教師可在孩子閱讀繪本時用以輔助其學習；學校單位亦可在對全校師生與家長做特教宣導時，先以繪本作引導，再以學習手冊作輔助，增進其相關特教知能；若班級剛好有新進的視覺障礙學生時，教師可以根據特殊需求學生個別化需求，尋找學習手冊內最適合當下情境的引導單或教學策略加以應用。

註：《犀犀的煩惱：學習手冊》可單獨添購，每本定價新台幣 50 元，意者請洽本
　　公司。

Something is Troubling Rhino

Written by Ying-Ru Meng &
Ming-Han Wang
Illustrated by Ning Yan
Translated by Arik Wu

My name is Rhino.

These are my friends.

They are very caring.

When I need to touch-read braille books, they will rush to help me turn to the right page, but sometimes they may press the braille characters too hard.

When I am thirsty, they will rush to help me open the water bottle.

When I am in class, they will rush to touch my special laptop out of curiosity.

When the call of nature comes, they will quickly come to take me to the toilet.

I am so glad to have them as my friends.

They make me happy, and my school life will never be complete without them.

However, something is troubling me, and I do not know how to tell my friends about it.

That is, whenever I want to move, the helping hands reaching from all directions actually confuse my sense of direction.

Whenever my classmates try to guide me through the classroom, I will always bump into something, mostly the desks and chairs that have been crashed from one place to another by them.

Moreover, they will help me whenever our teacher asks us to turn to a certain page. Sometimes they press the braille characters so hard that the embossments disappear. So I can no longer touch-read and have a hard time catching up with the lectures.

I am thankful for having these caring friends.

But I wish they could understand my real needs.

Before I entered in the school, my special education teacher had already given me a series of orientation and mobility training based on my learning and living environments.

So, as long as the environments are the same, I can move around freely.

If you want to guide me, please allow me to hold your arm or shoulder. I can recognize the direction through the motion of your body.

If you want to help me with turning pages, please do not press the braille characters. Instead, you can tell me the page number directly.

I love having you in my life.

I love having you around.

I love your passion.

I love it when you read me stories.

I love it when you share with me the joys and sorrows.

I am so happy to have you in my life!